Dogs and Birds Book 1:
Notes and Lesson Plans for Parents and Teachers

Elza and Chris Lusher

Animal symbol are Registered Community Designs
000188339 (0001-0022)
U.S. Design Patents D517593 S, D108088 S,
D18509 S-SD18512 S, D518850 S

Printed by Kingsley Print and Design Limited, Egham, Surrey

Contents

Section 1 – The Basic Elements of the Dogs and Birds Approach

Introduction

Dogs and Birds is a method which makes it possible to teach the piano/keyboard to children as young as three years old very successfully. It is *not* necessary for the child to know the alphabet. The method is also advantageous for older children since it dramatically speeds up the learning process and builds musicality. It can be used successfully for children up to the age of seven years old. There is a strong emphasis on singing whilst playing the keyboard – the method has its roots in the immensely successful approach to teaching children developed by the Hungarian Zoltán Kodály. As well as learning to play the piano/keyboard, the child will be able to sing and have a very solid foundation for further musical study.

The following resources are available from www.dogsandbirds.co.uk:

- Dogs and Birds Books 1 and 2 (in both Animal Notes and Blank Notes Editions)
- Dogs and Birds: Nursery Rhymes and Famous Melodies (in both Animal Notes and Blank Notes Editions)
- Notes to Book 1 for Parents and Teachers (these notes)
- A CD of the pieces and rhythm exercises in Book 1, included with these notes
- A set of small animal tiles and coloured staves
- A set of wooden animals and a large set of staves
- A manuscript book (with either 4 staves per page or 6 staves per page)
- A sheet of animal stickers (containing 7 sets of the 7 animals plus a few extra animals)
- A complete music set for beginners (with either small animal tiles or wooden animals).

This method is suitable for teaching children from three to seven years old, although in some cases even younger children may learn successfully. In general, the animal notes editions of the books are recommended for ages three to six and the blank notes editions are

1

recommended for ages six to seven. Very often the two editions are best used in parallel

Teaching Dogs and Birds

There are a number of ways to teach children using the Dogs and Birds approach and materials. One option is to arrange private piano lessons from a sympathetic teacher from the outset. However many parents might not wish to do this initially, especially if their children are very young. Some of these materials have been prepared in order to allow parents to work with (or teach) their children, even if they have had no previous musical experience. The video "The Dogs and Birds Piano Method in Action" gives a good introduction to the basic elements of the approach and can be found in the Video Demos section at www.dogsandbirds.co.uk and on the Dogs and Birds YouTube Channel at www.youtube.com/user/elzalusher.

It is possible for parents to teach the material in Book 1 to their children. Studying in this way will provide an enjoyable but strong musical foundation for those wishing to learn any instrument, including the piano. Book 2 is aimed at those wishing to continue their study of the keyboard or piano. The material in Book 2 is more advanced and for this it is really necessary to have lessons from a piano teacher. Of course if the parent has a solid background in the piano it might be possible to teach the material in Book 2 as well. The repertoire book, Dogs and Birds: Nursery Rhymes and Famous Melodies, is at a level somewhere between the two tutor books. Children can start using this towards the end of Book 1 and can continue using it in parallel as they finish Book 1 and start Book 2.

The principle behind this method is very simple for children to understand. This means that they can actually practise unaided between lessons. This is especially important for those of a young age. It makes lessons worthwhile since without daily practice the child might well forget melodies, rhythms and even the notes from one week to the next.

The CD, which contains all the pieces and rhythm exercises in Book 1, is extremely important for parents who are teaching their children – especially those parents without any previous musical background. The appropriate tracks must be listened to before each lesson. The CD can also be used to help children with their practice. You should try to copy the material on the CD as closely as possible. It is particularly important for the child always to sing, and not to play too fast. Please use the CD as a guide.

Using These Notes and Lesson Plans

These notes are written in order to help you get the most from working through Dogs and Birds Book 1. The material has been broken up into 17 "Steps". The term *steps* has been used rather than *lessons* since the amount of time needed for each step depends on the age and application of the child. Each step might take a few lessons or just one.

Each step consists of a set of exercises and games to play with the children to help them to learn the concepts. Since the exercises in the steps are often similar, the appropriate techniques will be explained in this introduction before detailing the various steps. The exercises are ordered differently in each step so as to add variety to the lessons. The method involves:
- marching and "tapping" the rhythm exercises in Book 1,
- playing and singing the musical pieces in Book 1,
- sung finger exercises, not included in Book 1,
- playing an echo game involving singing and pitch recognition,
- using the small animal tiles or wooden animals, and staves in various ways, including combining them with the echo game,
- making up stories about the illustrations in the book,
- improvising, by using the whole body and moving freely on the keyboard,
- simple composition, when the child is ready, possibly using the tiles and staves,
- drawing images using coloured pencils and paper inspired by the musical pieces, improvisations or compositions.

3

Sections 2 and 3 should definitely be followed by parents who wish to teach their children, but teachers may also find them useful. Section 2 describes how to carry out the musical exercises and games, and section 3 contains the steps.

Section 4 gives a set of ideas which may help if children are having problems with particular aspects of the approach. These tips can be especially useful for extremely young children.

Section 5 contains material written specifically for parents who have no previous musical experience. It explains the simple musical notation used in Book 1, shows how you can use animals to help find the notes on the piano keyboard and shows (with reference to Book 1) how these notes can be represented using musical notation. *Those without prior musical experience should read section 5 before working through section 3 (and the ideas in section 4) with their child.*

Section 6 contains notes for teachers, explaining some of the principles behind this approach and section 7 gives information about the CD.

Lesson Times
Typically a session with the child might last 30 minutes. This may seem a long time for a three, four or five year old to concentrate on one thing, however by breaking up each lesson into a series of smaller parts you will find that this amount of time is necessary – the time will fly by. Each step usually has five or six parts to it. It is recommended that you give the child enough time to master each step before going onto the next. There is no benefit to be gained from rushing the child – learning music should be an enjoyable and fun experience. In some cases, if parents are teaching their children at home, it might be better to split the lessons into shorter sessions, especially initially if the child's concentration span is short.

The Importance of Daily Practice
At this age short but *daily* practice is much more important than a longer period less frequently. You should find that with 5 minutes

every day (both singing and playing the pieces) the child will improve rapidly. You will see that the child's concentration span will increase noticeably.

Practice should be planned but varied. Each day the child should sing and play at least 2 pieces twice, and perform 2 elements of the step (for example rhythm exercises and improvisation, "tapping" and the echo game, or composition and finger exercises).

Small Animal Tiles and Coloured Staves
The 56 small tiles with animal pictures on them, can be placed either on the keyboard in the appropriate position or on the set of coloured staves. The back of the tiles are black so they can be turned over on the staves once the child knows the note. The treble clef and top lines on the staves are coloured red, and the bass clef and bottom lines are coloured blue. This is to help the child distinguish between the left and right hand. Generally you can mark the child's left and right hands in various ways, for example use a coloured marker to put a red spot on the right hand and a blue on the left, or make use of coloured ribbons or coloured elastic bands.

The tiles can be used for many different musical learning games, as will be explained in these notes and lesson plans:
- The tiles bring extra fun to the lesson and practice, and make learning notes even easier for the child. They can be turned over onto the black side as the child learns the note.
- Each set contains 7 sets of the 7 animals (Cat, Dog, Egg, Fish, Goose, Ant, Bird) plus an extra Cat, an extra Ant, an extra Bird and 4 extra Dogs.
- The tiles can be used from the first lesson, when the child needs to find all the Dogs on the keyboard.
- Together they help the child to learn the geography of the keyboard. There is an animal tile for every white key on a full-sized keyboard.
- They can be used for making up finger exercises, using the coloured staves.

- They help the child to realize that an animal can sit anywhere horizontally on its particular line or space.
- They can help with echo games, composition, improvisation, memory games, sight-singing, sight-reading and learning the position of the notes on the staves.
- There are enough animals to compose interesting tunes or to copy melodies from book 1 onto the staves.
- Each tile contains an animal character from the Nursery Rhymes and Famous Melodies book. All the characters are different, and children love to pick out which is which.

You can use Blu-Tack (or an equivalent adhesive putty) to stick the animal tiles onto the staves. The staves can then be placed on the piano in place of a musical score, enabling children to play melodies they have composed using the tiles.

The front cover of the staves shows the positions of the animals on the keyboard for the notes below and including middle C, and shows the position of the animals on the lines of the bass clef. The back cover shows the positions of the animals on the keyboard for the notes above and including middle C, and shows the position of the animals on the lines of the treble clef. The staves therefore act as a useful reminder for both student and parent.

Use of the Blank Notes Edition
There are two important differences between the animal notes and blank notes editions of Book 1. The musical pieces, rhythm exercises and illustrations are exactly the same in both editions. However the animal notes edition has animal symbols printed in the notes in order to aid note recognition, whereas the blank notes edition does not. Also in the animal notes edition the treble clef and the right (red) hand parts of the rhythm exercises are coloured red, and the bass clef and the left (blue) hand parts of the rhythm exercises are coloured blue – in the blank notes edition they are all black.

The blank notes edition can either be used on its own, or in parallel with the animal notes edition. It depends to some extent on the child. Some children (in particular the older ones) wish to learn from the blank notes edition. It is still vitally important that they sing the animal names of the notes as they play, in order to develop their inner ear. With younger children you can use the two editions in parallel and this should be encouraged. You can place both books on the piano, with the same pages next to each other. Ask the child to play a piece from the animal notes edition and subsequently to try to play the same piece from the blank notes edition. Do not remove the other book – it will act as a safety net. Another approach, which is sometimes useful, is to get the child to work through the animal notes edition and later on work through the blank notes edition.

In group teaching with mixed ability students it is possible for them to play the same piece together, with the stronger students using the blank notes edition.

Using a Manuscript Book
It is very important to keep a record of your lessons, and the easiest way to do this is to use a manuscript book. Here you can summarize the material covered lesson by lesson. It is much easier to keep track of what the children have learned and how well they are progressing by writing it down clearly.

You should always write into the manuscript book the rhythm exercises, pieces, finger exercises, and echo games etc. that the child should practice during the following week or days.

Later on you can use the manuscript book for writing down compositions or other written homework.

Manuscript books are available from www.dogsandbirds.co.uk with either four or six staves per page. Use the four stave manuscript book when studying Book 1.

Using the Animal Stickers
The animal stickers have been produced in the main for giving to the child as a reward for good work during lessons. The stickers are small enough to be stuck on the keys as an aid to learning. This is *not* a practice to be encouraged however, especially for children of five and over, who are usually quite capable of remembering the appropriate names of the keys easily. It can be tried with children under five to make the lessons more fun initially, but you should stop the practice as soon as it is possible. It could potentially slow down the child by developing a reliance on seeing the sticker in order to recognize the key. Sometimes it is necessary to use the stickers in this way, but they should only be used as an aid if the child is really having problems remembering.

If you do not have a set of small animal tiles, the stickers can be stuck onto card to create extra musical notes to use with the keyboard or the large set of staves.

A Suitable Keyboard
Since singing is an important part of this approach it is vital to have an instrument that is in tune. For the material in Book 1 a three to four octave keyboard is perfectly adequate. An electric keyboard will be perfectly in tune and therefore very suitable to sing with. If you would like to start teaching your three or four year old child to play the keyboard you might not initially wish to spend a lot of money to buy an instrument. At the present time the keyboards obtainable from music shops start at around £70-£80 and you might not wish to spend that sort of money. These instruments tend to be "all-singing, all-dancing", with many different instrument sounds and rhythms. These are good but somewhat unnecessary for teaching young children the basics of the keyboard. If you wish to see whether your child is interested in playing, you can probably find something cheaper by looking around. You might be able to find some good second-hand bargains.

Section 2 – The Components used in the Seventeen Steps
Rhythm Exercises

These exercises are dispersed throughout the book. It is quite common for very young children (under five years old) to find these harder than the musical pieces. However they are very important for the children in order to develop a strong sense of the beat, and they are excellent preparation for playing the musical pieces hands together. They really should not be overlooked. There are a number of ways the exercises can be carried out and you will find instructions in the steps below. They should *not* be carried out too fast. Something like one beat (one crotchet/quarter note) per second is ideal. A good way of "tapping" the rhythms is to get the children to use their palms to play many notes at once on the keyboard – low notes with the left hand and high notes with the right hand. They should play from the shoulder – this is very good for freeing up the arms, and they should count the beat aloud "One Two Three Four One Two Three Four etc." whilst "tapping". Use the CD as a guide if required.

Very young children often struggle initially with co-ordination in the rhythm exercises. They find it difficult to play different rhythms in the two hands. Many have difficulty distinguishing between left and right, and top and bottom. For this reason, in the animal notes edition of Book 1 the right hand parts of the rhythm exercises are coloured red and the left hand parts blue. You can make a little red mark on the child's right hand and a blue mark on the left hand with marker pens, or put red and blue rubber bands or ribbons around the wrists. This should make a big difference.

If the child still has difficulty then the teacher or parent should try tapping the top or bottom line while the child taps the other line. In this case you should COUNT together.

It will be necessary to develop the child's inner pulse. This can be improved by marching, clapping or drumming daily. These activities all play a very important part in establishing good rhythm. If you practise EVEN and controlled marching with your child then you can help to develop a solid inner pulse, guaranteeing the natural development of rhythm.

Musical Pieces
It is essential that the child sings the melody whilst playing the pieces and you should always encourage this. You should start by singing the melody before playing (if possible) and get the child to sing with you. You should sing using the animal names. If you have difficulty in sight-singing a piece, first listen to the CD in order to familiarize yourself with it, and then play the melody on the keyboard whilst singing it. Children might be reluctant to sing at first. However if you persevere with this, especially if you always sing as well each time a new melody is introduced, they should become quite confident within a few lessons and happily sing on their own. Your child should always begin each piece by counting in one bar as is done on the CD.

Usually young children find it difficult to sing the G or F below middle C (see section 5 for an explanation of the musical notation). If this is the case then you might ask the child to sing the melody an octave higher than written. Listen to "Aquarium" (track 40 of the CD) for an example.

Sung Finger Exercises
These additional exercises are important in that they:
- prepare the child for playing the pieces,
- provide good ear-training,
- improve the child's singing ability,
- strengthen the fingers,
- introduce the geography of the piano,
- prepare for improvisation or composition.

Since these exercises are not printed in Book 1 you should write them out in the manuscript book, in order to keep track of where you are. If the child cannot yet read or write you may need to draw animal symbols to symbolize the notes. As well as using the exercises in these notes, you can also make up your own. The small animal tiles and coloured staves can be used for composing simple finger exercises, as described later.

Make sure that the child can play through each exercise before attempting to play the piece that follows in a particular step. Generally below age five children should use the "Owl's Eyes and "Owl's Glasses" finger positions, as described later, in the section "Recommended Finger Positions for Different Ages". Children should play from the shoulders – moving their whole arm as a unit. In order to see how this should be done ask them to draw a series of arches (like a viaduct) on top of the keyboard, hands separately. Their arms should be free, without any tension. Children have a tendency to raise their shoulders and keep their elbows close in to their waists. Therefore please ensure that they keep their elbows away from the body, with their shoulders down. For fun you can mention that they should play as if they have hedgehogs under their armpits which mustn't be harmed. Also make certain that they do not just play from their elbow or wrist – the movement should start from the shoulder. Each note should be detached and not played legato (smoothly). Their wrists should not be dropped (in order to allow space for a mouse to run under their hands).

Children should always sing the animal names out loud whilst playing. Throughout these notes upward facing stems on minims and crotchets are used to signify notes to be played with the right hand and downward facing stems signify notes to be played with the left hand. These exercises should be played at each octave on the keyboard, with the children always singing at the octave which is most comfortable for them (probably around middle C). If the keyboard has many octaves then they should play these exercises in a standing position and walk along the piano in order to reach the required notes. Sing with the children in order to encourage them.

It is good practice to ask students to try playing the finger exercises with their eyes closed, or to look up at the ceiling as they play. This will allow them to feel the spacing of the notes on the keyboard and

11

help them ultimately to look at the music, rather than relying on looking at their hands whilst playing.

The Echo Game

The echo game involves playing notes at random on the keyboard and asking the child to identify which is which, singing them back using the animal names. If you have a set of small animal tiles or wooden animals (see below) you should always use them as you play the echo game (as described later). An example of the echo game is given in step 2. There you are asked to play Dogs and Birds randomly. You should play the notes in a number of different octaves in order to train the children's ear, although they should always sing the pitch that is comfortable for them. Gradually in the steps that follow more notes are added. Relatively quickly you should find that the children are able to distinguish between the different notes. Really occasionally children find this challenging, especially once the number of notes increases. If this is the case you might wish to start with them simply singing or humming the notes back before identifying them by name.

If the child has problems with this game at the beginning then try another way to train the ear. Play two "Dogs" of different pitches and ask the child to identify which note is high and which is low. You can do similar exercises as you add more notes. Always make sure that the child can hear whether notes are moving up or down before you start to introduce difficult sequences.

Small Animal Tiles/Wooden Animals

As well as the small animal tiles, a set of wooden animals is available for use with this method, as is a large set of staves. Each set contains one of each of the seven animals. The animals can be placed on either the keyboard or the large staves. For the exercises in the seventeen steps you can use either small animal tiles or wooden animals. You should ask the child to place the animals in the correct place on the keyboard or the staves. You can call each stave a set of shelves, a staircase, or a block of flats for example, or you can tell the child that 𝄞

symbolizes a house in the mountains and $\mathbf{\vartheta}$: a house in the valley. Another way is to liken the top stave to five red benches and the bottom to five blue benches in a school. Some children need to sit on red benches, others on blue. And some need to stand between the benches.

It is particularly important that you do the exercises with the animals and staves since if children are using the animal notes edition it is possible for them to play the music by looking at the animals without actually realizing on what line or space a particular animal sits. You can also use animals and staves as you play the echo game. This is very good both for ear training and visualization of the notes, and it helps to make learning more interesting.

You can watch examples of animals and staves in use in the Musical Exercises and Games section of the Video Demos at www.dogsandbirds.co.uk, and also on the Dogs and Birds Piano Method YouTube channel at www.youtube.com/user/elzalusher.

When you have introduced all of the notes you can play a game with a dice. Place an animal on the stave then roll the dice and based on the result get the child to add the appropriate animal in its correct position. It is good to ask the child to sing the animal name at the correct pitch then check it by playing the note on the piano. A throw of 1 corresponds to the same animal, 2 to the next animal note etc.

Combining the Echo Game with the Animals and Staves
We take as an example the exercises in step 2, where the children are introduced to the Dog and the Bird. You should sit at the piano and get the child to sit in front of the open staves. Play and sing "Dog Bird Dog" and ask the child to echo this by singing it back. Then play either Dog or Bird and ask the child to identify it. The child should recognize which note you have played and sing it back with its appropriate name and pitch, at the same time putting the correct animal in its proper place on the staves. Now again play either Dog or Bird. The child should sing the appropriate animal name and pitch and either place the correct animal on the staves or remove it if it is there already. If you are using

13

the tiles then just place another animal on the staves. Continue the game by playing randomly either Dog or Bird. This is extremely good for ear training and also for teaching the child the correct positioning of the notes on the staves.

If the child has difficulty with this game initially you can try a simpler version of this exercise. First place the Dog and Bird in their correct positions on the staves. Then play Dog and Bird randomly and ask the child to point at the appropriate animal (either with a stick or a pencil) as they sing its name. Once the child can do this then you can progress to the harder version of the game.

If you find that the children can do this exercise easily then you can try playing Dog or Bird one octave higher or lower. Always ask them to sing back at the pitch most comfortable for them (probably that closest to middle C).

You can also build up sequences of Dog and Bird. For example play "Dog Dog Bird Bird Dog Dog Bird" and ask the children to sing the phrase back with the appropriate names, pointing to the correct animal as they sing. The level of difficulty of the sequences you can use will depend on the child. Try to challenge him or her somewhat, but not too much. Make sure that the child can master the challenge and feel successful.

Continue with the game in a similar manner as you add more notes. Finally the child will be able to remember and sing back 4 to 6 note melodies and point to the notes while singing.

Stories

Each piece in the book has a title and is illustrated. A story runs through the book. Please feel free to elaborate on this and discuss it with the child, using the illustrations as a guide. This helps to stimulate further the interest and imagination of the child and makes the lessons more fun and enjoyable. It is very advantageous to talk about the illustrations since it brings the child closer to the pieces and the music.

Improvisation

For some time during each lesson children should be allowed to express themselves on the keyboard, by "playing" a story. This is the time when they can bang on the keyboard freely, or stroke it softly depending on the story they make up. It is also an excellent time for children to have a break and stand up from the piano stool and stretch their bodies. The story could perhaps describe their favourite fairy tale, a game with their pet or friends – practically any aspect of their life. In the first few steps some ideas are given. You should help by suggesting themes, but make sure this activity is kept under control. Keep a strict time limit. Make sure your child uses a great variety of sounds and touch – for example soft or loud, long or short, single notes or groups of notes, hands together or separately, smooth or detached, etc. You can ask the child to draw coloured images using coloured pencils and paper, depicting the stories used in the improvisations. This helps them to express themselves more fully.

Composition

In addition to these exercises and games the child will sometimes be asked to compose a short piece under your guidance. Try to compose music similar to that which the child has already learnt, or use the sung finger exercises as a basis for the composition. This is an excellent use for the small animal tiles and coloured staves. Children can write out their compositions using the animals and staves and then place the staves on the piano to play them.

Recommended Finger Positions for Different Ages

Very young children (those below about five years of age) will probably have relatively weak fingers. In this case it is recommended for them to play notes with the side of the thumb, supported by the index finger (or later on the middle finger). To produce this hand position, ask them to form "Owl's Eyes" with their hands. The thumb and index fingers should form circles (which the child can look through like spectacles), with the 3rd, 4th and 5th fingers held higher up forming the owl's eyelashes. They can then play notes with the sides of the thumbs keeping the same hand position. Initially they should use this finger position to play Dog and Egg with the right (red) hand and Bird and Ant with the left (blue) hand when they meet these notes in both the musical pieces and the sung finger exercises. The short video "The Dogs and Birds Piano Method in Action" (to be found at www.dogsandbirds.co.uk) shows an example of this finger position. Young children should also use the "Owl's Glasses" finger position. This is similar to the "Owl's Eyes", but has the thumb and middle fingers forming circles. Again play the keys with the sides of the thumbs. This finger position should first be used when playing Goose with the blue hand. These finger positions will (a) support the thumbs whilst playing, (b) help develop a good hand position with curved fingers and (c) evolve naturally into the use of the 1st, 2nd and 3rd fingers at a later stage. Of course older children, with stronger fingers should be able to use their 1st, 2nd or 3rd fingers, as appropriate, from the start.

Balancing the Elements

All the elements discussed in this section are important for children in order to become rounded musicians. In general children will be better at some elements than others. If, for example, tapping the rhythm exercises is weak, playing the musical pieces hands together is difficult, or carrying out the listening games is hard do not worry. Practise, watch the child, and use the ideas outlined in this book to make the particular element more interesting.

If something is complicated or hard for the children try to solve it from a different angle. Please do not force anything! For example, if they are reluctant to sing initially then you should sing continuously and ask them to copy you or just sing along with you. If they have difficulty with rhythm then try many different ways to achieve your goal – use pieces of paper or names of vehicles (see later) to describe lengths of notes, try marching, clapping or barking, or other techniques, as outlined in these notes. If their hand positions are weak then you should first determine if they are ready for a proper hand position, or whether it is better use the "Owl's Eyes" and "Owl's Glasses" finger positions described above. Maybe start to do preparatory work away from the piano to achieve the correct hand position – ask them to hold their heads or kneecaps with curved fingers. Also you can concentrate more on the correct hand position and correct fingering when carrying out the sung finger exercises.

The most important thing is to motivate the children, and each child is different so you will need to find out what works in each particular case. For some children making the lessons fun is the most important thing. In other cases you can fire their imaginations by telling stories. You might use finger puppets to help with your descriptions. For others at this young age, filling the lessons with kindness, love and care is the key to opening the children. You should always make sure that the children will be successful so give them exercises that will be challenging but possible, and make the lessons varied. Work together with the children to produce happy, stimulating and successful lessons.

Video Demos

Examples of the various activities described above can be seen on the Dogs and Birds Piano Method YouTube channel which can be found at www.youtube.com/user/elzalusher. Before starting to teach Dogs and Birds it is recommended in particular that you watch the video "The Dogs and Birds Piano Method in Action", which gives a summary of the approach.

Section 3 – The Seventeen Steps

STEP 1

Improvisation – Before you open Dogs and Birds you should explain to the child that music is wonderful for expressing feelings and moods, and it can describe many different pictures and stories. In order to demonstrate this you should do the following improvisation exercises on the piano and get the child to repeat them.

First play LOW, LOUD, LONG notes – these represent the *elephant*. Do this with your hands, playing many notes simultaneously – first one hand and then the other, as if you are walking side to side on the bass notes.

Now walk all the way up the keyboard softly. These SOFT, LONG notes increasing in pitch represent a *cat* walking. At the very end hit your hand hard on LOW BASS notes to illustrate the cat jumping down from the fence it has been creeping along. You can then do a similar thing on the black keys as well, representing a *black cat*.

You can describe happy *birdsong* by playing HIGH, LOUD, SHORT notes. Do this by turning your hands with a rotary motion from the wrists. Play with the backs of your hands – both hands simultaneously, using a rocking movement.

Listen to track 1 of the CD for examples of these first three improvisation exercises.

Finding the First Note – When the student is ready, turn to page 1 of the book and ask him or her to find all the Dogs on the keyboard. Put a Dog tile (or pencil) on top of each of these Dogs – you need one tile/pencil for each of the Ds on the keyboard. If you are using the toy wooden animals then place the wooden Dog on each of the Ds in turn. Get the child to play the notes with the thumbs, and sing "Dog". Make sure that all the fingers are above the keyboard, and curved if the child is ready for that. If the child is under five years old, then it may be

18

easier to use the "Owl's Eyes" finger position, holding the index fingers and thumbs together like spectacles whilst playing with the sides of the thumbs (as described on page 15 of these notes).

Sung Finger Exercise – Ask the child to play:

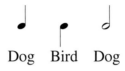

Dog   Bird   Dog

Use the right hand thumb or the "Owl's Eyes" finger position to play the Dog and the left hand thumb or "Owl's Eyes" to play the Bird. Remember that the children should play from their shoulders, moving their whole arm – they should not just play from the elbow or wrist. It is important that they sing "Dog Bird Dog" whilst playing the notes. You should perform this exercise at each octave on the keyboard, but always sing around middle C i.e. the pitch that is most comfortable for the child. There is an example of this on track 1 of the CD.

Musical Pieces (Page 3) – First sing "Playground" together with the child, using the animal names i.e. Dog Dog Bird Bird Dog Dog Bird etc. If necessary listen to the CD first and then play the melody on the keyboard whilst singing it. Parents without previous musical experience should see "Important Notes for Parents" (section 5 of these notes) for advice and instruction. If the child is very young and has no experience of reading from left to right then hold a pencil together and point out the notes as you sing. This will teach the child to read and helps with concentration.

After singing the line then get the child to play and sing. Repeat the same procedure with "By the Lake". Children should possibly use their thumbs to play these notes – the right-hand thumb for the Dog and the left-hand thumb for the Bird, or use the "Owl's Eyes" finger position. They should play from the shoulders – moving the whole arm. Advice on a proper hand position is given in section 5.

Rhythm Exercises (Page 2) – These are the first rhythm exercises. Rhythm exercises are dispersed throughout the book and they are very important for the child in order to develop a strong sense of the beat. The child and teacher/parent should march, clap and count the rhythms. Marching helps the student to feel an even beat. Most of the rhythm exercises have four beats in a bar, so the child and teacher/parent should count "1 2 3 4 | 1 2 3 4 | 1 2 3 4 | ...". As you clap try to emphasis the first beat of each bar.

Using Cars to Explain the Lengths of Notes – If children have difficulty understanding the lengths of the notes then use the chart on the back cover of Book 1 in order to aid understanding. A car takes up less space in a car park than a bus. The black notes (crotchets/quarter notes) have a length of one beat, the white notes with stems (minims/half notes) last for two beats, and the white notes without stems (semibreves/whole notes) last for four beats. The same applies to notes when they are written on a musical stave. If children are unable to count then ask them to clap or tap the rhythm on the back of the book, whilst saying aloud the words:
"Car Car Car Car | Big-Car Big-Car | Car Car Big-Car | Very-Very-Big-Bus".

You should use these words with the children in the rhythm exercises (especially with extremely young children), until they are ready to count using numbers. Further suggestions for teaching very young children are given in section 4.

= rhythm exercise
- Park @ diff octaves

STEP 2

Rhythm Exercises (Page 4) – In these and the remaining rhythm exercises the child should "tap" the rhythms and count the beat using numbers (or cars if necessary). This should be done by striking the keys with open palms as described before, in section 2. Hand symbols indicate which hand should be used. When a note is written directly above another note then the notes should be played (or tapped) at the same time. If the beat is not yet even the child and teacher/parent should march as in step 1 until the beat becomes strong. It is a good idea to listen to a clock ticking and ask the child to count and clap to the ticks.

Sung Finger Exercise – Sing and play:

Dog   Dog   Bird   Bird   Dog

Play this at each octave on the keyboard as described earlier, always singing (at a comfortable pitch). If possible once children have played this ask them to play it again with their eyes closed.

Stories – Never miss an opportunity to make up stories about the illustrations. For example in "In the Bush" and "Cotton Flower" (page 6) you can talk about the nest, which is being prepared for the next new note (the Egg). Please go through the story with your child. A story always enables the child to find links that help the learning process.

Musical Pieces (Pages 5 and 6) – Play and sing "Sparklers", "Wait until it is Dark", "In the Bush" and "Cotton Flower". Do this in a similar manner to earlier, that is singing first and then playing and singing.

The Echo Game – Now play the echo game. This involves playing Dogs and Birds at random on the keyboard and asking the child to identify which is which and sing them back using the animal names. Remember to play these notes in a number of different octaves.

Small Animal Tiles/Wooden Animals – Get the child to put the animals in their correct places on the keyboard and then place them on the appropriate places on the staves. It is often easier for the child if you call the stave a ladder or stairs. The Dog lives on the top (or red) ladder and the Bird lives on the bottom (or blue) ladder – or the Dog lives in a mountain home and the Bird lives in a house in the valley.

The animals and staves can be linked with the echo game to provide an excellent opportunity for ear training. Get the child to place the Dog and the Bird on the staves. Play and sing "Dog", then play and sing "Bird". After that play just one of them and ask the child to identify it by removing the appropriate note from the staves. Then play a note again. Ask the child to identify it, either by removing a note from the staves or putting it back on the staves in its appropriate place. With practice the child will soon be able to distinguish notes with ease. This game can be extended to more notes later.

Improvisation – Here you should ask the children whether they can think of a story to describe by playing on the keyboard. If not, suggest a theme for them to improvise. You could try to express different moods, for example being happy, sad, sleepy, angry, lively etc. It is important to discuss the different moods with the children. Ask them to tell you which situations make them happy, and which make them sad, for example. Remember that you can stimulate the children's imaginations by asking them to draw pictures with coloured pencils and paper.

Composition – If you have the animal tiles and coloured staves make up a simple melody using the notes you already know and then sing it as you play it on the piano.

STEP 3

Improvisation – Make up a new story and play it on the keyboard. This time the student should use both hands whilst playing or should play together with the parent or teacher. Play LOUD and SOFT notes, and LONG and SHORT notes. Together with the child think of situations when you need to be LOUD or QUIET and describe them using the piano.

Musical Pieces (Page 7) – Sing and play "Promise to Behave". Perhaps you can try playing this piece from the Blank Notes Edition, or try to play it from memory.

Stories – Look at the picture on pages 8 and 9, and discuss it with the child. Explain that the Eggs must all be on the bottom line of the staves. Where is the Dog sitting?

Small Animal Tiles/Wooden Animals – Use the animals Dog, Bird and Egg to teach the child their positions on the keyboard and the staves. Maybe link this with the echo game as described in the previous step, or with the sung finger exercise below.

Sung Finger Exercise – Sing and play:

Dog   Egg   Dog   Bird

Rhythm Exercises (Page 8) – Tap these rhythms with alternate hands counting aloud as you do so. Please do not forget to march if it is still necessary.

Musical Pieces – In "Tightrope" (page 9) you can ask the child to count "1 2 3 4 | 1 2 3 4 | 1 2 3 4 | ..." rather than singing the animal names whilst playing this piece. Sing and play the pieces on page 10. If the child is ready then use the second (index) finger for Egg, otherwise play Dog and Egg with the "Owl's Eyes" finger position. When playing "Far-off Hills" and "Egg Rock" just use the right hand. Do not play anything smoothly (legato) – play separated notes using the whole arm.

STEP 4

Stories – Talk about the picture on pages 10 and 11 with the child. The Dog and Bird are looking for the Egg Rock in the secret garden, when there is a full moon. Can you see the swan constellation in the sky? In this and in all cases make the pieces more interesting by talking about the stories in the pictures.

Musical Pieces – Sing and play "When the Moon is Full" and "The Secret Garden" (page 11), and "Golden Rings" (page 13).

The Echo Game – Play the echo game with Dog and Egg. Maybe also introduce Bird occasionally. As before play the note and ask the child to identify it and sing it.

Small Animal Tiles/Wooden Animals – Use the animals once more, placing them in turn on the keyboard and the staves. Again link this exercise with the echo game. Place the Dog, the Egg and the Bird on the staves initially. Play and sing these three notes in turn. Now play a single note and ask the child to identify the note as explained in step 2. Continue this process. Try to challenge the child gradually.

Rhythm Exercises (Page 12). Tap exercises 4a, 4b and 4c.

Improvisation – Make up another story. A possible story is about a snake climbing up a tree to catch a bird at the top. The bird in the tree is the same as in the first lesson. Is the bird caught by the snake or does it escape? Move your wrist and elbow from side to side like a snake slithering, pressing down as you slide up the keyboard. What happens next will depend on your answer. Then get the child to repeat this story.

Sung Finger Exercise – Sing and play:

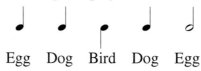

Now try to repeat it with your eyes closed.

STEP 5

Musical Pieces – Sing first and then play and sing "Rug from Morocco" (page 13) and "The Forest Comes Alive" (page 14).

Sung Finger Exercise – Sing and play:

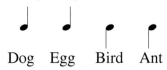

using the thumbs for Dog and Bird and the index fingers for Egg and Ant. Please use curved index fingers if possible. Play with detached notes, using your arms. If the child's fingers are still too weak for this then they should use the "Owl's Eyes" finger position.

Musical Pieces – Sing and play "Desert" (page 14) using the second finger of the left hand (curved if possible), or use "Owl's Eyes".

Improvisation – Make up a story or use the following one. A frog is jumping happily at the lakeside. A fish calls her for a secret meeting the following day. They meet at 3 o'clock and they swim together to the bottom of the lake where they investigate the hidden treasure that the fish had found earlier.

The Echo Game – Play the echo game with Bird and Ant. Possibly add Dog as well. Do not make this too difficult. Combine this with the small animal tiles or wooden animals if you have them.

Stories – Talk about the picture on pages 14 and 15. Point out that the Ants are marching along the blue path and the Eggs on the red. What is happening in the King's Palace?

Musical Pieces – Play "A Safe Path" (page 15) with the left hand only. Use detached notes, because in general at this stage children's fingers and hands are not yet strong enough to play legato.

Rhythm Exercises – Tap exercise 4d on page 12, and exercises 5a and 5b on page 16.

STEP 6

The Echo Game – Play the echo game with Bird, Ant and Dog. Maybe add Egg as well, if the child can distinguish the notes easily. If not then make it as simple as possible. Use Dog and Bird plus one other animal (Egg or Ant).

Sung Finger Exercise – Sing and play the exercise below or make up your own exercise using the same animals.

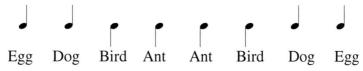

| Egg | Dog | Bird | Ant | Ant | Bird | Dog | Egg |

Rhythm Exercises – Tap page 16 exercises 5c and 5d.

Stories – Discuss the picture on pages 16 and 17. The animals are now out in the mountains. Possibly they will stay out all night. It is very clear in the mountains and they can see the Milky Way in the sky.

Musical Pieces – Ask the child to try to sing "Open Gate" (page 15) before playing it. If this is difficult then use the piano to check the notes. Also try this with "Watch the Milky Way" and "Great Smoky Mountain" (page 17).

Small Animal Tiles/Wooden Animals – Use the tiles or wooden animals. Find their places on the keyboard and on the staves. Link this with the echo game, if you haven't done so already.

Improvisation – Make up your own story, or improvise a story about a lost baby Kangaroo. You can then ask the child to use coloured pencils or crayons to illustrate the story on paper.

Composition – Using the animal tiles (or by drawing animals in the manuscript book) make up a melody using Egg, Dog, Bird and Ant. The child should then play and sing it on the piano. Ask the child which notes he or she can remember, then turn these over to the black side and play and sing the piece again.

27

STEP 7

Stories – "Trick on You" is a hard piece. It is tricky because there are no long notes where the child can rest. There is no time to wonder. You should concentrate now! Who will do the trick with the rabbit? Will Goose learn to somersault between the top two blue ropes?

Musical Pieces – Sing and play "Stop Your Wondering" and "Trick on You" (page 18).

Sung Finger Exercise – With the addition of a new note (the Goose), the five notes the child now knows form a *pentatonic scale*. Using both hands play and sing:

| Egg | Dog | Bird | Ant | Goose |

If the child is ready then get him or her to use the middle (3rd) finger for the Goose (curved if possible). Make sure that the child still uses detached notes and uses the whole arm. If the child is still using "Owl's Eyes" fingers then use "Owl's Glasses" for the Goose, using the thumb and middle finger as described on page 16 of these notes.

Musical Pieces – Using only the left hand play and sing "Picnic Basket" and "Somersault" (page 19).

Rhythm Exercises – Tap exercises 6a and 6b on page 20.

Improvisation or Composition – Try making up a new story. For example, "Walking on a rainy day". You can use the music to describe raindrops (in the park or forest), your steps, your partner's steps (friend, parent or pet), thunder, heavy rain, a rain storm, and finally a rainbow and sunshine. Alternatively you could start to make up your own music in a more structured way. If possible write it down in the manuscript book. If the child is younger and not yet ready for this you can use the small animal tiles and coloured staves. Watch the video "The Dogs and

Birds Piano Method in Action" for ideas. There you can see Milana and Elza making up a composition together.

The Echo Game – Play the echo game with Goose, Bird and Dog. You can link ear-training with movement. For example, children should touch their toes if they hear a Goose, stand up straight if they hear a Bird, and stretch their arms up high if they hear a Dog. You can see Hanhan doing this in the "Dogs and Birds Piano Method in Action" video at www.youtube.com/elzalusher. Alternatively you can use the wooden animals or tiles, and staves with the echo game.

STEP 8

Rhythm Exercises – Tap exercises 6c and 6d on page 20. To make sure that the beat is even your teacher, parent or other helper can add a steady beat. If the tapping is still difficult your helper can point at the rhythm in the book and help by calling out words such as Red, Blue, Hold, Both.

The Echo Game – Play the echo game with Goose, Bird, Dog and Egg. You should always introduce the notes to the child before playing any melody. For example play and sing Egg Dog Bird Goose and ask the child to sing this phrase twice before starting the game. Repeat this throughout the game before playing each sequence of notes. If the child finds this difficult then don't play all the notes in a single phrase. Just play two different notes at a time. [For example play Dog Bird, then Dog Egg, then Egg Dog, followed by Bird Goose.]

Improvisation or Composition – Improvise a story based on the child's favourite activity. Alternatively, compose a melody similar to that in step 7. If the child is ready then you can add rhythm and bar lines as Fiona does in the video "The Dogs and Birds Piano Method in Action". Do this using a whiteboard pen on the coloured staves. Fiona is using quavers/eighth notes that the child will not yet know. However after placing the appropriate animal tiles on the staves you can draw a "stick" to represent a crotchet/quarter note, an oval around the tile and a stick to represent a minim/half note, and an oval around the note to represent a semibreve/whole note.

Musical Pieces – Sing and Play "Take Your Partner" and "Sunday Afternoon" (page 21), and "Skipping Stones" (page 23). The semibreve/whole note is used for the first time in "Sunday Afternoon". Once again please talk about the illustrations in order to make the pieces even more interesting for the child. Why do the animals have to cross the river? Possibly they have arranged to meet the bird there.

Small Animal Tiles/Wooden Animals – Do not forget to use the tiles or wooden animals. You can use the animals and the staves to help with the composition, or you can link them with the echo game as usual. You can also make up other ways to use the tiles and staves to help with the children's score reading. For example you can ask them to place all the Eggs, Dogs, Birds, Ants and Geese onto the staves.

Sung Finger Exercise – Play with hands *together* and sing the *left* hand notes:

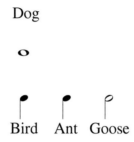

The right hand should play the Dog at the same time as the left hand plays the Bird. If the child is very young and finds this difficult to do then start with a long Dog in the right hand then add Bird, Ant and Goose in the left hand. Maybe you can use the "Owl's Glasses" finger position for every note. This and the next few sung finger exercises will help the child to prepare for playing musical pieces with *hands together*.

STEP 9

Rhythm Exercises – Clap or tap the rhythm exercises on page 22 SLOWLY with an EVEN beat. Please make sure that the third beat is *not* longer than the others. The "dot" following a note increases its length by half as much again. Therefore a dotted minim/half note has a length of 3 beats rather than 2. It is recommended to give a strong stress on the 1st beat of the bar and to clap or tap the 2nd and 3rd beats as SOFTLY as possible.

Composition – Make up a composition using either the manuscript book or the animal tiles and coloured staves. Try to make up a piece with 3 beats in a bar, clearly marking the bar lines.

Sung Finger Exercise – Play hands together and sing the *right* hand part:

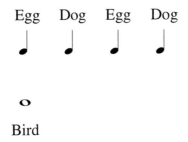

The left hand should play the Bird at the same time as the right hand plays the first Egg. Hold the Bird down for four beats.

Musical Pieces – Sing, then sing and play "Wheelbarrow" (page 23), "Tea Time" (page 24) and "Forbidden City (Page 25). Talk about the pictures as before. Our friends have now arrived in China and have been invited to have Jasmine tea with the Emperor. Their appointment is in the Forbidden City.

The Echo Game – Play the echo game with Goose, Ant and Bird. Maybe you can combine this with the tiles or wooden animals here, but still focus on singing.

Improvisation – This can now be made more structured. The phrase

Goose   Dog   Goose   Dog   Bird

can either be repeated as an echo or changed to become an answer:

Goose   Dog   Goose   Dog   Goose

You can either play a "question" phrase and ask the child to provide the "answer", or ask the child to devise both question and answer. Usually the question phrase is "open" and the answer phrase "closed" as below:

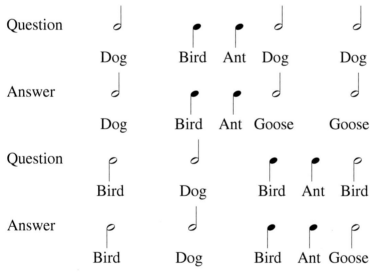

Question

Dog   Bird   Ant   Dog   Dog

Answer

Dog   Bird   Ant   Goose   Goose

Question

Bird   Dog   Bird   Ant   Bird

Answer

Bird   Dog   Bird   Ant   Goose

The answer phases may differ from these.

33

STEP 10

The Echo Game – Play the echo game with Ant, Dog and Egg. If this is easy then you can add Goose.

Composition – Get the child to make up a melody with 3 beats in a bar in the right hand and add a simple accompaniment in the left hand.

Rhythm Exercises – Tap exercises 8a and 8b on page 28.

Small Animal Tiles/Wooden Animals – Play with the tiles or wooden animals on the keyboard and staves. Use them for your composition and link them with the echo game.

Musical Pieces – Sing and play "Chinese Pagoda" (page 26). This has a complicated rhythm known as syncopation. The child must feel this syncopated rhythm whilst counting or playing. To help with this initially you can just tap and count this piece or count the melody, instead of singing the animals.

Musical Pieces (left hand only) – Play and sing the left hand parts of "Hands Together" and "Traffic Jam" (page 29).

Sung Finger Exercise – play with hands *together* and sing the left hand notes:

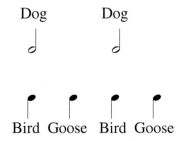

The right hand should play the Dogs at the same time as the left hand plays the Birds, since the Dogs are written directly above the Birds.

STEP 11

Musical Pieces – Play "Hands Together" and "Traffic Jam" (page 29) with both hands and sing the left hand part as you do this. Play and sing *only* the left hand part of "Welcome to My Home" (page 30).

Rhythm Exercises – Tap and count page 28, exercises 8c and 8d.

Sung Finger Exercise – play with hands *together* and sing the left hand notes:

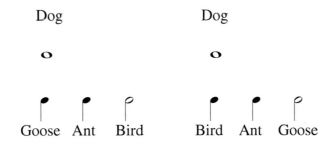

If your child is willing to make up his or her own finger exercises then you should encourage this. Possibly you can combine use of the animals and staves, and the sung finger exercises at this stage.

The Echo Game – Play the echo game with Goose, Bird, Dog and Egg.

Small Animal Tiles/Wooden Animals – Place the tiles or wooden animals you have learnt up to now on the keyboard and on the staves. These are Goose, Ant, Bird, Dog and Egg. As you play the notes on the keyboard, ask the child to sing them back and place the correct animals on the appropriate place on the staves. The child must not forget to sing.

Musical Pieces – COUNT and play "Night after Night" (page 27). Be very careful with the beat in this piece. The 3rd beat must *not* be longer than the 1st and 2nd beats in each bar. Very young children are often not ready to keep an even beat with 3 in a bar. Learn this piece in 2 or 3 weeks' time if your child has difficulty with it now.

STEP 12

Musical Pieces – Sing and play "Welcome to My Home" (page 30), adding the long "D". Then play "Dreamy Head" (page 30) both hands together and sing the left hand part.

Stories – You should discuss the picture on pages 30 and 31. The Ants are taking the corn to the Winter Palace. Who is it for? For the Prince or Princess? Who lives in the palace? How far away is it? Why is it called the Winter Palace?

Musical Pieces – Play hands separately and sing "Winter Palace" and "Crush the Corn" (page 31). Sing the melody using the animal names or sing the beat numbers to the melody.

Rhythm Exercises – Tap page 33, exercises 9a and 9b.

Sung Finger Exercise – Play hands together and sing the right hand part:

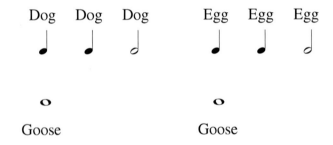

Use third fingers only all through the exercise, or use the "Owl's Glasses" finger position. The Goose in the left hand should be played simultaneously with the first Dog and the first Egg in the right hand.

The Echo Game – Play the echo game with Goose, Ant, Bird and Dog, possibly using the wooden animals or tiles, and staves as earlier.

Small Animal Tiles/Wooden Animals – Use the tiles or wooden animals, getting the child to put them on the coloured staves, and link this with the echo game.

Improvisation – This is probably the time to ask the child to improvise a structured melody. Use a "question and answer" approach. For example you might play:

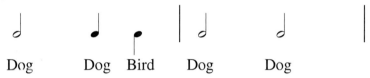

Dog   Dog Bird   Dog   Dog

and the child might answer with:

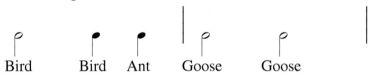

Bird   Bird Ant   Goose   Goose

If children are not yet ready for this then ask them to improvise a rhythm clapping the "answer" to your rhythm "question" and/or you could just ask them to ECHO back exactly the same melody that you sung or played. Counting and singing are always a big help if difficulties occur.

STEP 13

Musical Pieces – Play "Winter Palace" (page 31) with hands *together* and sing the melody. Then do the same with "Crush the Corn" (page 31). Play "Jack and His Men" (page 32) with hands *separately* and COUNT.

Stories – Look at the picture on page 32 and 33. Try to work out who lives in each house. Why does one house have so many windows?

Rhythm Exercises – Tap page 33, exercises 9c and 9d.

Musical Pieces – Sing first, then sing and play "Stick and Hat Stomp" (page 34). Make sure that the Cat is played with the left hand in this piece, as is indicated in the book.

Sung Finger Exercise – Play in a detached way and sing:

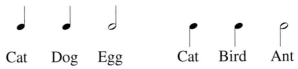

Either use fingers 1, 2, 3, or "Owl's Eyes", "Owl's Eyes", "Owl's Glasses", first in the red hand and then in the blue hand.

Small Animal Tiles/Wooden Animals – Place the appropriate tiles or wooden animal in their places on the keyboard and on the staves. Make sure that the child understands the middle C position and the continuity between the two staves.

The Echo Game – Play the echo game with Cat, Dog and Egg. You can link this with the wooden animals or tiles, and staves. If the child finds this easy then you play Cat Dog and Egg one octave higher or lower, or add Goose.

Improvisation – Improvise a story on the keyboard or improvise a simple duet (with student and teacher/parent). Make sure you count together and play at the same tempo (speed). You can use melodies from the finger exercises and those you have used for the echo games. Please make it simple!

STEP 14

Musical Pieces – Play "Jack and His Men" (page 32) hands together and COUNT as you sing the left hand melody. After this try to sing the left hand melody without playing it but play the right hand part at the same time.

Musical Pieces – Play "Hop on My Back" (page 35) and "Floating By" (page 37). Approach these pieces in the following way. First play the parts hands separately i.e. sing and play the right hand part, then count and play the left hand part. Once both parts are known very well hands separately you can then ask the student to play them hands together. Always sing or count the melody when you play hands together.

If children can sing the melodies very well then you can ask them to sing the melody (without playing it) whilst accompanying themselves with the left hand. See the video "The Dogs and Birds Piano Method in Action", where Hanhan performs this "two-part singing".

Rhythm Exercises – Tap page 36, exercises 10a and 10b.

Sung Finger Exercise – Play and sing hands separately:

First play this with the right hand at all octaves on the piano. Then repeat the same exercise using the left hand, again at all octaves on the piano. If this is easy then the child should practise SKIPs hands separately. See page 50 of these notes for an explanation of skips. By this stage the child should understand moving up and moving down on the piano. Moving from Cat to Egg is a skip up and moving from Cat to Ant is a skip down. You can tell the child that a skip is moving to the neighbour's neighbour. Start with a Dog and then play F, A, C, E ..., singing "Dog, skip up, skip up, skip up ..." . Move up the piano as far as you like. Then start with a Dog followed by B, G, E, C ..., and sing "Dog, skip down, skip down, skip down ...". Perform these finger

39

exercises first with the right hand and then with the left hand, using either the 3rd fingers or the "Owl's Glasses" finger position.

The Echo Game – Play the echo game with Ant, Cat and Egg. Make sure to use the wooden animals or tiles, and staves. If this is easy then make it longer or add more animals.

Composition – Compose a piece similar to "Jack and his Men". It should have the melody in the left hand, with the right hand accompanying.

STEP 15

Small Animal Tiles/Wooden Animals – Place the tiles or wooden animals on the keyboard and the staves as usual. Focus on both Fishes and both Geese.

Musical Pieces – Play "Old MacDonald" (page 38) and sing the animal names of the notes. "Da Capo al Fine" means go back to the beginning and end at "Fine" without the repeat.

Sung Finger Exercise – Sing and play:

First play this with the left hand at all octaves on the piano. Then repeat the exercise using the right hand, again at all octaves on the piano. If this is easy then you can practise STEPs hands separately. See page 50 of these notes for an explanation of steps. Cat to Dog is a step up and Cat to Bird is a step down. Tell the child a step is a move from an animal to its neighbour. Start with a Dog then play E, F, G, A ..." and sing "Dog, step up, step up, step up ...". Then start with a Dog followed by C, B, A ..." and sing "Dog, step down, step down, step down ...". Do these exercises first with the right hand then with the left hand. You can try to play these notes with the 4th finger if the child can manage that, or hold the thumb and 4th fingers together and play with the side of the thumb. You can call this finger position the "Owl's Goggles". This might be too hard, in which case use the "Owl's Glasses".

Composition – Make up your own piece with 4 beats in a bar. The melody should be in the right hand, with a simple accompaniment in the left hand.

Musical Pieces – Sing and play "Aquarium" (page 40). If children struggle with the low Fish then possibly they can sing the melody an octave higher, as on the CD. By this stage children often like to attempt to sing the low note even if they cannot quite make it – this is fine.

Musical Pieces – Approach "Wishing Well" (page 42) in the following way. Play each part hands separately, COUNTING whilst you play the right hand and SINGING the melody whilst you play the left hand. You will ask the child to play the piece hands together in step 16.

Rhythm Exercises – Tap page 36, exercises 10c and 10d.

The Echo Game – Play the echo game in the bass clef with F, A and middle C. Possibly it is advisable to use the small animal tiles or wooden animals.

STEP 16

The Echo Game – Play the echo game with Cat, Dog, Egg and Goose. If the child is able to then you can try even more notes. Reinforce this by using the wooden animals or small animal tiles, and staves.

Musical Pieces – Play "Wishing Well" (page 42) hands together. Try this at first by counting as you play and then by singing as you play. Then play and sing "Transposition" (page 41). Make sure that the child understands that this is the same melody as in "Aquarium".

Rhythm Exercises – Tap page 39, exercises 11a and 11b.

Sung Finger Exercise – Play and sing:

| Dog | Dog | Egg | Egg | Fish | Fish |

Here the notes played in the right hand (stems up) should be played an octave higher than those played in the left hand (stems down).

Composition – Give a title to one of your earlier compositions or to a new one. Just as the pieces in the book are illustrated, you should draw a picture describing this composition using coloured pencils and paper.

Small Animal Tiles/Wooden Animals – Place the tiles or wooden animals appropriately on the keyboard and the staves. Now that the children know all of the notes please explain to them that the animals "Cat, Dog, Egg, Fish, Goose, Ant, Bird" keep repeating both on the staves and on the keyboard in different pitches.

Musical Pieces – Before you play "All Over the Universe" (pages 44 and 45), play and sing the first line, making sure your child can keep an even beat – COUNT if necessary. Then sing the red hand part of the second line and the left hand part of the third line. This is the melody. Sing the left hand melody an octave higher if necessary, as is done on the CD. Do not forget to talk about this picture. In general children are fascinated by it and love to talk about it.

STEP 17

Sung Finger Exercise – Play hands *separately* and sing:

Cat   Dog   Egg   Fish Goose

First play this with the right hand at all octaves on the piano. Then repeat the same exercise using the left hand, again at all octaves on the piano. If the child is ready then you can vary the melody, rhythm or hands. Either use 3rd fingers or "Owl's Glasses" for each note.

Musical Pieces – Play and sing "Jingle Bells" (page 43). This music is repeated. The first time you play the two bars that have the number 1 above them and the second time you play the two bars that have a number 2 above them instead. If the children love this piece then try to get them to play it from memory. They should sing the animal names.

Composition – Compose a simple piece, give it a title and learn to play it from memory.

Rhythm Exercises – Tap page 39, exercises 11c and 11d.

Musical Pieces – Play "All Over the Universe" (pages 44 and 45) hands together. Do this first whilst counting and then whilst singing the animal names. As you play either sing the melody using beats or the animal names.

Small Animal Tiles/Wooden Animals – Place the tiles or wooden animals on both the keyboard and on the staves in the appropriate positions. Once again make sure that the child understands clearly the repeating pattern of the animals on both the keyboard and the staves.

The Echo Game – Play the echo game with Cat, Dog, Egg, Fish and Goose. This is usually quite hard for the students – miss out one or two notes if necessary, or make the order of the notes simple (that is do not use tricky intervals). You can again use the wooden animals or tiles.

Section 4 – Some Helpful Tips to Make Things Easier, in Particular for Very Young Children

In some cases it is possible to use the Dogs and Birds method with children younger than four. Parental help is usually essential in these situations and if the child is having lessons it is good if the parent attends. This section contains further tips that will help when teaching very young children. They are also useful for slightly older children, if they are having difficulty with specific aspects of the approach. In particular, the small animal tiles and coloured staves are important when working with older children as well. They constitute a "board game", which the children love to play, and which speeds up note recognition and memorizing significantly.

Further use of the Small Animal Tiles and Coloured Staves

The animal tiles and coloured staves are especially useful for the very young. There is an animal for every white key on a full size piano keyboard. The child can therefore use the tiles to find all the Dogs on the keyboard (placing the Dog tiles in appropriate positions), and similarly for the other animals when you introduce them. The animal tiles can also be placed on the coloured staves, with Blu-Tack (or an equivalent adhesive putty). Since the front and back "covers" of the staves show the correct positions of the animals both on the keyboard and the lines of the staves children can turn over the board to check their answers. Also, by looking at the covers parents can easily see the correct positions, even if they have limited musical experience.

Sometimes it is important to emphasize to the child that you read music horizontally and not vertically. For example only the Dog can sit just below the first line on the treble clef. This can be demonstrated very easily if you have a whole set of Dogs. Ask your child to place 5 or so Dogs in a row in the correct position on the staves. They should then play them on the piano and sing. This exercise can be repeated as you add more animals. The child can also use the tiles and staves to make up new finger exercises to try on the piano, and to compose new melodies.

Using the Coloured Staves on the Piano in Place of the Score

In some cases it is possible to help very young children to learn to read music by turning the tiles and staves into a musical score. You can "compose" music in front of their eyes for them to play. This helps in particular with learning the position of the notes on the staves. The staves can be placed on the piano instead of the music. During the first five or so lessons very young children can often read more easily from this "score" than they can from the music in the tutor book. Form a simple melody (for example with Dogs and Birds) using the tiles, and stick them onto the staves with Blu-Tack. Then ask the child to play the melody on the keyboard and sing. You can then form another tune and ask the child to play and sing that. This technique can be very helpful, especially with the very young. You can continue to use this approach as you compose finger exercises and pieces.

Since the tiles are black on the back they can be turned over when the child is confident of the position of the note. This in some sense simulates moving from the animal notes edition to the blank notes edition of the book.

A Variation on the Listening Game for the Very Young

Very young children might not be able to point out the position of the Dog and the Bird on the large set of staves when you play the ear-training games. This may happen because they do not understand the concept of the exercise. If this is the case then you should place a Dog tile or wooden Dog in their right hand and a Bird tile or wooden Bird in their left. When you play a Dog or a Bird, they should raise up the hand containing the animal they recognize by the sound. Watch the ear-training part of the "Dogs and Birds Piano Method in Action" video to see how Milana learns to do this on her first piano lesson. You can say that the Dog and Bird are talking with each other. The children are therefore indicating which of them is speaking at a given time. You can even bark when you play a Dog and tweet when you play a Bird.

Various Techniques to Help with Rhythm

If children are very young (three years old or younger) it may be that they don't understand the difference between a Car and a Big-Car. In that case it can help if together with the child you draw a Car, a Big-Car and a Very-Very-Big-Bus. You can see examples on the back cover of Book 1. If that doesn't work you can use small rectangles of white and black paper to symbolize minims/half notes and crotchets/quarter notes. Make the white pieces of paper twice as long but the same width as the black pieces of paper. Form a series of long and short notes using the pieces of paper. Then "tap" this series on the keyboard, together with the children, saying aloud "Short Short Long | Long Short Short", for example. Hold their hands as they "tap" with their palms as explained in step 2. It is better to tap a long note than to clap it since you can make the note sound for two beats. You can also ask them to compose some rhythmic phrases using the pieces of paper and then tap and say them as earlier. If you have access to a photocopier you can produce black paper by opening the lid and pressing "copy".

Another trick is to ask the children to "bark" the rhythm. Really very young children might find counting or using vehicles too hard, yet they might well be able to bark the beat:
"woof woof woof woof | woof woof woof woof ".
Combine this with clapping whilst barking a steady beat continuously. Hold a crotchet/quarter note for one woof, a minim/half note for two and a semibreve/whole note for four.

When teaching children to tap the rhythm exercises hands together you can call out various words to aid them as they tap, for example Red, Blue, Both, Hold.

If a child has difficulty tapping rhythm hands together (for example exercise 4d on page 12), it can help to tap the rhythm exercise with him or her while sitting opposite one another. Only focus on the difficult bars (for example the first and last bars in exercise 4d) and slow down the beat. If you have a drum, sit facing each other with the drum in between and tap the rhythm on it. Or you could sit at opposite sides of a

47

small table and tap on the table top. You will have to tap the "mirror image" of course, swapping left and right hands, however tapping together can make it much easier for the child.

Helping Children by Pointing out Notes with Your Fingers

When children start playing the musical pieces, it can be very helpful if at the beginning you use your fingers to point out the notes on the musical score as they play. This technique is even more beneficial when tapping the rhythm exercises. If you count aloud (SLOWLY) and follow the notes from left to right, using your left hand, you can use your middle finger (maybe marked with red) to help read the top line and your index finger (maybe marked blue) to help with the bottom line. The easiest way to describe this is to say that the fingers should "walk" along the music (from left to right) with the middle finger touching the top notes and the index finger touching the bottom notes when they should be tapped. In general at any given point in Book 1 the rhythm exercises are more complicated than the pieces and may require more practice. This is because the rhythm exercises are a preparation for later pieces. You can also help with the musical pieces by pointing with a pencil. You and the children should hold the pencil together and point as you sight-sing the piece. For very young children you should use the right (red) hand to point out notes in the $\oint$ line and the left (blue) hand to point out notes in the $\mathcal{I}$: line.

Walking on the Staves

Another way of helping young children to remember the positions of the notes on the staves is to allow them to walk on the large set of staves. This can work for very young children – and they love to do it. Or you can make your own stave with five strips of ribbon, for example taped to the floor. As you play notes on the piano get your child to step on the appropriate line or space. It is best to teach the lines first because it is easier for the child to walk on one line without touching any other. To start with play Egg Egg Egg Egg on the piano and ask your child to step on the first line. Then play Goose Goose Goose Goose. After that play Egg Goose Egg Goose ... You should always make sure that your child sings with the steps. You can also use the animal names to label the lines. For example you can call the first line in the treble clef the Egg line and the second line the Goose line. If you are limited in space then you can do a similar thing with just one line and practice just three notes. You can call the line, for example, the Ant line. The Bird will be above the line and the Goose below. This exercise is hard for very young children, who might not have a good sense of balance.

An Alternative Order for the Pieces in Book 1

Very young children sometimes have difficulty playing with both hands simultaneously (i.e. hands together). If this is the case then it is recommended to change the order of the pieces. This situation first occurs in the piece "Hands Together". Avoid these pieces and continue playing the pieces where this does not occur – "Stick and Hat Stomp" (page 34), "Old MacDonald" (page 38) and "Jingle Bells" (page 43). You can also play "Aquarium" (page 40) and "Transposition" (page 41), which only have simultaneous notes in the last bar. In this way the child will learn the Cat and the Fish. Meanwhile focus systematically on the rhythm exercises (which are extremely important for helping the child to play pieces hands together) and on playing finger exercises hands together. One common problem is that if children play two notes simultaneously on the keyboard (by putting the fingers down at the same time) they then want to remove them from the keyboard at the same time. One way to avoid this tendency (and to help the children to "feel" what it is like to play two notes at once) is to create special finger exercises. For example ask the children to play a long Dog in the right (red) hand and keep it held down whilst playing other notes freely with the left (blue) hand. Start the Dog before playing the other notes. Or you can start by playing a long Goose in the left hand and improvise freely above it with the right hand. The key to being able to play hands together well is to do lots of finger exercises. You can link this strongly with composition, possibly using the small animal tiles and coloured staves.

Once the children have become proficient in doing rhythm exercises and finger exercises hands together you can then work through the pieces on pages 29 to 32, 35, 37, 42 and 44.

This highlights the importance of the rhythm exercises. As mentioned in section 2, very young children often find the rhythm exercises harder than the pieces, and there could be a tendency to miss them out. Please avoid this tendency since mastering the rhythm exercises is vital in developing a good sense of beat and pulse.

The Transition from Animal Notes to Blank Notes

Sometimes children are reluctant to change from the Animal Notes to the Blank Notes Edition. It is possible for children to play the pieces just using the animals, without fully understanding the position of the animal on the staves, although using the tiles or wooden animals, and staves should help with this. However, if you have progressed towards the end of the book and the children are still having difficulties, you can start to teach steps and skips. Throughout Book 1 only the white notes on the keyboard are used. In this case a step is the distance between a line and a space on the staves, which corresponds to moving from one white key to the adjacent white key, and a skip is the distance between two lines or two spaces on the staves, which corresponds to jumping over the adjacent key to the next nearest white key. Examples of skips are moving up from Bird to Dog or moving down from Bird to Goose. Children should know by this stage that moving up on the staves corresponds to going to the right on the keyboard and moving down on the staves corresponds to going to the left.

At first you should practise with the children just on the keyboard. The connection with the notation will come naturally at a later stage. The Teacher or Parent should play a Dog, say "Step Up" then play an Egg; say "Step Up" then play a Fish; say "Step Up" then play a Goose. Continue slowly and systematically in this manner, asking the children to repeat what you are doing. Gradually they will begin to understand the process, and soon you will be able to teach "Step Down". Once they have mastered this, you can try something else, for example a skip, or repeating the same note. Introduce everything very slowly, making sure they understand one concept completely before introducing the next.

Bringing a Toy Animal or Doll to Visit the Animals

A very good stimulus for young children is for them to bring a favourite toy, for example a rabbit or a mouse, or a favourite doll to "visit" the musical animals. This can be a finger puppet or cuddly toy. Or they could bring a toy car or bicycle for the animals to ride. You can say, "Let's take your toy to visit the Dog. Where does the Dog live?" Knock on the piano (as if knocking on the door of the house) and then get the child to put a Dog tile or wooden Dog on a "D" and bring the toy to it. Or go to visit the Fish. Does the Fish have enough water in his tank? You can do a similar thing with the staves rather than the keyboard. These games can work well, and serve to fire the children's imaginations.

A Copying Game

Possibly after a few weeks of improvisation the children would like to try something new. The copying game can be introduced as a replacement for improvisation. You should get them to play groups of 4 to 6 notes together on the keyboard using open palms. Play with both the right and left hands and play from the shoulder – this is excellent for learning to play with free arms. You should play all the notes simultaneously. This may be noisy, but children love it!

First the parent or teacher should play and the child should copy. Then, after a while, switch around, so that the child plays first and the parent or teacher copies. Just vary what is played, for example a series of long and short sounds, or loud and soft, or high and low. Talk about what you are playing. You can also mix the elements as the child gets more proficient. This is a good exercise for improving concentration and memory, as well teaching many elements of music.

Playing the Echo Game without Notation

You can start ear-training without using any notation. This will become useful later on for improvisation or for playing a well-known melody by ear.

Play a simple sequence of Dogs and Birds on the piano, for example Bird Dog Bird Bird or Dog Bird Bird Dog. Ask the children to play and sing it back straight away. If they find this easy then you can add rhythm as well to this echo game, for example Long-Dog Long-Dog Short-Bird Short-Bird Long-Dog. Gradually you can add more and more notes, but make sure that the children can always perform the exercise easily. As long as they are successful they will want to do more and more of these exercises. You need not worry about which fingers to use. Let the children do whatever they are comfortable with.

Although you may need to give a lot of help initially, as the children become more confident you can make the phrases longer and make the melodies more complicated.

Another Variation on the Listening Game and the Echo Game

You can ask children to make up and play a simple melody. You then need to play this melody back. If you deliberately make some mistakes when you play it back the children will have great fun spotting these.

Making use of New Technology

If the children's parents have a smartphone or tablet then it is good to download a mini-piano. The children can then do ear-training or practise the echo game in the park, in the car, when waiting for something, or even when they are away on holiday. There are many options, for example "Pianist" for the iPhone or "Pianist Pro" for the iPad.

Section 5 – Important Notes for Parents

Hand Position and Posture
When playing the keyboard it is important to work towards a correct hand position and good posture from the start, thereby avoiding getting into bad habits.

The extent to which you can achieve a correct hand position depends on the child. If the child's hands are ready to form a proper hand position you should encourage this, however please do not be too strict. For children with less well-developed hands it is important that they strike the keys in a comfortable way. Very young children you should use the "Owl's Eyes" and "Owl's Glasses" finger positions as described on pages 15 and 16 of these notes.

You should ask the children to hold their heads in their hands, like a ball. This should produce the correct hand position with curved fingers. When playing use the tips of the fingers and the side of the thumb, with the palm facing down.

You should always try to get the best out of the children. Therefore if they are able to hold their hands firmly with curved fingers then always remind them to do so. However if they are having problems with pitch, rhythm, sitting or reading the symbols as well as with hand position then you have to be a bit more flexible. You should approach their problems systematically and try to ensure that the children are always successful. Do not force anything. When developing the hand position and posture make sure that all the fingers are above the keys and the palms are facing down, not sideways, and that the arms are free. You should make sure that the elbows are comfortably far from the body and that the shoulders are not pushed up. Tell the children that they should imagine that they have hedgehogs under their armpits that they shouldn't squash. You should avoid any tension in the children. Their heels should be on the floor – put something firm underneath if their legs are too short. They must not cross their legs. It is also important that children should always sit with a straight back and should not push their wrists up or down when playing. The lower arm should be level with or slightly above the keyboard.

Musical Notation

The Names of the Notes

In music a note of a certain pitch is given a name and conventionally letters are used. There are 88 keys (both black and white) on a full size piano, corresponding to 88 different pitches, however there are *not* 88 different names. The notes are divided into groups, with 12 pitches (seven white keys and five black keys) in each group. Look at the keyboard and find this repeating pattern of keys. In Book 1 only white notes are used and seven names (C, D, E, F, G, A, B) are needed to describe them. Therefore each letter will occur more than once on the keyboard. This same pattern of white notes is repeated all the way along the keyboard.

Since young children find it difficult to remember letters, in Dogs and Birds the notes are represented by animal symbols – with which the children should be very familiar already. The seven names now become Cat, Dog, Egg, Fish, Goose, Ant, Bird. Each animal has specific places both on the keyboard and on the musical staves (the sets of five lines used to notate music). The positions the animals (or letters) occupy on the keyboard is shown on the back page of Book 1. For example, the first note that children should learn is D – the Dog. The Dog "lives" between the two black keys on the keyboard. This is by far the easiest white note for children to recognize, which is why the Dogs and Birds method starts there.

Immediately to the left of the Dog on the keyboard is the Cat – C, and the C that is closest to the centre of the keyboard is called "middle C". In this book the position of middle C on the musical staves is right in the centre of the two sets of 5 lines. The best example of this can be found on page 38 – "Old MacDonald".

Beats and Note Lengths

The speed of a piece of music is determined by the beat, which is the basic unit of time. You should establish the beat before you start to play a piece, as you will hear on the CD. The beats must be even all through the piece. You should ask students to play, sing or count with a beat corresponding to a time interval of about one second, as you will hear on the CD.

In music the length of a note is as important as its pitch. The lengths of notes are measured in beats. Four different note symbols are used in this book. The longest note is the white note without a stem. This is called a semibreve in the UK and a whole note in the US. In all of the music in this book the semibreve has a length of 4 beats. The white notes with the stems (minims/half notes) are 2 beats long. Putting a "dot" immediately after a note increases its length by half as much again. Therefore a dotted minim has a length of 3 beats rather than 2. The black notes (crotchets/quarter notes) have a length of 1 beat. The lengths of the notes are represented pictorially on the back page of Book 1.

The Octave

The most important musical interval (the difference in pitch between two sounds) is the octave. For example C to the next C (above or below), or D to the next D etc. is an interval of one octave. In order to play the pieces in Book 1 your keyboard should have at least three octaves – it may have as many as seven and a half.

The Musical Staves and the Clefs

A typical line of keyboard music consists of two staves, each of five horizontal lines, joined together. See for example the music on page 3. In all of the music in Book 1 the right hand should be used to play the notes on the upper staff (or stave) and the left hand should be used to play the notes on the lower staff. Notes between the staves should be played with the right hand if the stem on the note points up and with the left hand if the stem points down.

The symbols at the start of each line of music are the treble and bass clefs. The treble clef is on the upper staff and the bass clef on the lower. The clefs are important in that they determine where the animals sit on the staves. For example the Dog sits under the bottom line when the treble clef is used (i.e. the upper staff for the music in Book 1) and the Bird sits above the top line when the bass clef is used. Coloured hand symbols are used to show which hand should play the notes on a particular staff, with the right hand in red and the left hand in blue. These hand symbols are not conventional and will not be found in ordinary music.

Bar Lines
All music is divided into short sections called bars (or measures in the US), each containing a well-defined number of beats. Most of the pieces in this book have four beats in a bar, however later on some music with three beats in a bar is introduced. The number of beats in a bar is important since it determines the character of the piece. For example a march has four beats in a bar whereas a waltz has three beats. The vertical lines separating notes that you can see in both the rhythm exercises and the musical pieces are called bar lines.

Repeat Marks
The two vertical lines with dots (which can occur anywhere on a stave) are repeat marks (see for example page 3). They signify that the phrase has to be repeated. If the music is not to be repeated the piece will end with double vertical lines, but without the dots (for example on page 24).

First and Second Time Bars
In "Jingle Bells" on page 43 the music is repeated with an alternative ending. First the music is played through to the end of the bars labelled 1 but after repeating, these two bars are replaced by the bars labelled 2. To make it easier for the child you can call these the first and second exits. For example you can leave a house by the front door or the back door (but not by both at once).

56

Da Capo al Fine
In "Old MacDonald" on page 38 the first line is repeated before going on to the second line. The "Da Capo al Fine" marking means that students should go back to the beginning of the piece and play until the "Fine" marking. This time they should not repeat the first line.

Section 6 – Additional Explanatory Notes for Teachers

Rests and Time Signatures

It was decided not to use musical rests in Book 1 since it is harder for the child to keep the beat if rests are included. They are introduced in Book 2. In addition time signatures are not used. At this stage they are an unnecessary complication for the students.

Quavers

Throughout Book 1 quavers have been avoided. In order to establish a good technique on the piano it is important never to play too fast initially and children tend to rush quavers. Their lengths are shown on the back cover of Book 2, however this is the only reference to them there.

Quavers are introduced in Dogs and Birds: Nursery Rhymes and Famous Melodies. Here both the rhythms and the speeds of the pieces are well-known. It is appropriate to use quavers in this case.

Finger Numbers

Finger numbers are not used in Book 1. They are introduced immediately at the start of Book 2. In the Dogs and Birds approach the child learns to associate the notes with animal symbols rather than finger numbers. If children learn to associate notes with finger numbers (as is the case with most tutor books) this can later cause reading problems as more than ten notes are introduced. This problem is avoided completely by using the animal symbols.

Group Teaching

The different elements discussed here can easily be carried out in a group context. Children can learn to sing and play the keyboard together. A great advantage of the Dogs and Birds method for group teaching is that animal notes and blank notes editions can be used in parallel as required, depending on the abilities of each of the children. You can also cater for those with learning difficulties by putting the animal stickers on the keys.

58

Section 7 – CD Tracks and Credits

Tracks

Track 1 of the CD contains an introduction which is followed by examples of sung finger exercises, simple improvisation exercises and the echo game. Each subsequent track number on the CD corresponds to the identical page number in Book 1. For example the rhythm exercises on page 2 of the book are on track 2, and "Playground" and "By the Lake", which are on page 3 of the book are on track 3. This makes it very easy to find any musical piece or rhythm exercise in the book – just go to the track that corresponds to the page you are on.

Credits

Keyboard: Elza Lusher
Voice: Ameera Gill and Parisa McCarthy
Recording and mixing: Jeff Ross